iMath
Readers

Herding a Hundred:
Counting the Sheep

by Donna Loughran

Content Consultant
David T. Hughes
Mathematics Curriculum Specialist

NORWOOD HOUSE PRESS
Chicago, IL

Norwood House Press
PO Box 316598
Chicago, IL 60631

For information regarding Norwood House Press, please visit our website at
www.norwoodhousepress.com or call 866-565-2900.

Special thanks to: Heidi Doyle
Production Management: Six Red Marbles
Editors: Linda Bullock and Kendra Muntz
Printed in Heshan City, Guangdong, China. 208N—012013

Library of Congress Cataloging–in-Publication Data

Loughran, Donna, author.

Herding a hundred: counting the sheep/by Donna Loughran and Linda Bullock;
consultant David Hughes, mathematics curriculum specialist.
pages cm.—(iMath)

Summary: "Mathematical concepts of counting, estimating, and "greater
than" or "less than" are introduced as readers help a farmer herd his sheep.
Readers learn to count using tally marks, hundred charts, and group counting.
Includes a discover activity, science connection, and mathematical vocabulary
introduction"—Provided by publisher.

Audience: 6–9
Audience: K to grade 3

Includes bibliographical references and index.

ISBN 978-1-59953-547-0 (library edition: alk. paper)
ISBN 978-1-60357-516-4 (ebook)

1.Counting—Juvenile literature.
2. Mathematics—Terminology—Juvenile literature. I. Bullock, Linda, author. II. Title.

QA113.L68 2013
513.2'11—dc23
2012023816

CONTENTS

Note to Caregivers:

Throughout this book, many questions are posed to the reader. Some are open-ended and ask what the reader thinks. Discuss these questions with your child and guide him or her in thinking through the possible answers and outcomes. There are also questions posed which have a specific answer. Encourage your child to read through the text to determine the correct answer. Most importantly, encourage answers grounded in reality while also allowing imaginations to soar. Information to help support you as you share the book with your child is provided in the back in the **Additional Notes** section.

Bold words are defined in the glossary in the back of the book.

Baaaaah!

Look at the woolly sheep standing in a row. Some of the sheep are white. Some are brown. And one has spots.

The sheep are different colors. And they are all hungry! How many hungry sheep do you count in the row? Count one by one.

One. Two. Three.
Keep counting. How many sheep do you count in all?

In this book, you will learn different ways to count. You will count to be sure that no sheep are missing!

Many Sheep to Count

Imagine you are a sheep rancher. You own 100 sheep!

They roam everywhere to eat. How can you count so many?

Why do ranchers count their sheep? They want to be sure they have all of them.

Idea 1: Count the sheep one by one. Are you ready? 1, 2, 3, 4, 5. What number comes next?

You can use a **hundred chart** to help you.

Hundred Chart

1	2	3	4	5	6	7	8	9	10
11	12	13	14	15	16	17	18	19	20
21	22	23	24	25	26	27	28	29	30
31	32	33	34	35	36	37	38	39	40
41	42	43	44	45	46	47	48	49	50
51	52	53	54	55	56	57	58	59	60
61	62	63	64	65	66	67	68	69	70
71	72	73	74	75	76	77	78	79	80
81	82	83	84	85	86	87	88	89	90
91	92	93	94	95	96	97	98	99	100

Idea 2: Keep a **tally chart**. Make a mark for each sheep you count.

Idea 3: Skip count. You skip count when you count by a number **greater than** one. Try skip counting by 2. Are you ready? 2, 4, 6, 8, 10. What number comes next?

What other numbers can you skip count by? How will you count the sheep?

Discover Activity

Materials
- a box
- 100 crayons

How Many Crayons?

Count 100 crayons. Put them in a pile. Then, close your eyes. Pick up some crayons from the pile. Put them in a different pile.

Now, open your eyes. Look closely at the two piles of crayons. What do you notice?

Which pile has more crayons? Take a guess. Then, count to check your guess.

Hundred Chart

1	2	3	4	5	6	7	8	9	10
11	12	13	14	15	16	17	18	19	20
21	22	23	24	25	26	27	28	29	30
31	32	33	34	35	36	37	38	39	40
41	42	43	44	45	46	47	48	49	50
51	52	53	54	55	56	57	58	59	60
61	62	63	64	65	66	67	68	69	70
71	72	73	74	75	76	77	78	79	80
81	82	83	84	85	86	87	88	89	90
91	92	93	94	95	96	97	98	99	100

How can a hundred chart help you count?

Is the number of crayons in the first pile greater than or **less than** the number of crayons in the second pile?

Using Groups to Count

You can **estimate** the size of a flock. You can tell about how many sheep there are in all.

But you must count to know exactly how many sheep are in the flock. One way to count is to count equal groups.

A **group** has two or more things in it. **Equal groups** have the same number of things in them.

A group of sheep is called a flock, a herd, and a mob. Which name do you like best?

Look at the picture above. How many equal groups of sheep can you make?

How Does Grouping Help You Count?

Look at the picture. It shows a carton of eggs. The way the eggs are put in the carton makes a **pattern**. A pattern is the way things repeat. Here, there are two groups of three eggs.

There is another pattern, too. There are three groups of two eggs. How many eggs are in the carton? Skip count to find the answer.

This carton holds even more eggs. What patterns do you see?

How many eggs are there in all?

How did you count them?

Show how you can skip count the eggs by 5.

What other numbers could you skip count by?

Check your answer on the next page.

Think about what you know.

There are six groups of eggs.

There are five eggs in each group.

How many eggs are there in all? Use the hundred chart to help you skip count by 5:

5, 10, 15, 20, 25, 30.

Hundred Chart

1	2	3	4	5	6	7	8	9	10
11	12	13	14	15	16	17	18	19	20
21	22	23	24	25	26	27	28	29	30
31	32	33	34	35	36	37	38	39	40
41	42	43	44	45	46	47	48	49	50
51	52	53	54	55	56	57	58	59	60
61	62	63	64	65	66	67	68	69	70
71	72	73	74	75	76	77	78	79	80
81	82	83	84	85	86	87	88	89	90
91	92	93	94	95	96	97	98	99	100

There are 30 eggs in all.

How is counting by 5 different from counting by 1?

A sheep eats plants.

Connecting to Science

Chew before you swallow. Have you ever heard that?

You eat. You chew. You swallow. The food goes to your stomach.

Your stomach is a pouch. It holds the food you eat. It adds juices. Then, it squeezes. Squeezing turns the food into a thick soup. Then, the stomach squeezes the soup out to a new part of your body.

A sheep eats, too. But it does not chew first like you do. No one can tell a sheep to chew before it swallows!

The sheep swallows food whole. The food goes into a stomach. But a sheep's stomach has four parts!

Part one squeezes the food into the second part. There, balls of cud form.

The cud goes back up to the sheep's mouth. The sheep chews the cud and then swallows again. This time, the food goes through the last two parts of the stomach.

Sometimes, people "chew the cud" with their friends. What do you think this means?

Math at Work

A Sheep Rancher's Work

Sheep need food and water to live. Sometimes, they need medicine. And sometimes, they need a haircut!

Each spring, sheep ranchers cut their sheep's wool. One sheep may lose 10 pounds of wool in one haircut!

Imagine that you give 10 sheep a haircut. You cut off 10 pounds of wool from each sheep. How many pounds of wool do you cut off in all?

Why do you think ranchers give their sheep haircuts in the spring?

Count the Sheep

How would you count sheep as they go in or out of a barn?

Sheep ranchers have another job, too. They must keep their sheep safe from bad weather and from animals that hurt them.

Sometimes, dogs help keep sheep safe.

Some ranchers also bring their sheep into pens or barns each night.

? What's the Word?

Have you met Russell the sheep? He lives in Frogsbottom Field. Russell is not like other sheep. You can find out why and read about Russell's adventures in books by Rob Scotton.

The sun is setting. Night is coming.

Your dog herds 50 sheep into a pen. You count as they go in. Then, you count 50 more sheep as they go into a second pen. Are any of your sheep missing?

You get up before the sun rises. It is time to take the sheep to the fields.

You have 4 fields.

25 sheep go in the first field.

25 sheep go in the second field.

25 sheep go in the third field.

25 sheep go in the fourth field.

Are any of your sheep missing?

Could a hundred chart help you count how many sheep there are in all?

Hundred Chart

1	2	3	4	5	6	7	8	9	10
11	12	13	14	15	16	17	18	19	20
21	22	23	24	25	26	27	28	29	30
31	32	33	34	35	36	37	38	39	40
41	42	43	44	45	46	47	48	49	50
51	52	53	54	55	56	57	58	59	60
61	62	63	64	65	66	67	68	69	70
71	72	73	74	75	76	77	78	79	80
81	82	83	84	85	86	87	88	89	90
91	92	93	94	95	96	97	98	99	100

Now night is coming again. The dog starts his work herding the sheep. Did any get away today? Let's count!

How will you count?

1. Will you **count** the sheep one by one?

2. Will you keep a **tally chart**?

3. Will you **skip count**?

Running sheep are hard to count!

Idea 1: Counting one by one will work. But the sheep keep moving!

Idea 2: Making tally marks will work. But you have nothing to write with.

Idea 3: Skip counting makes counting faster. And you do not need something to write with. Try that.

25 sheep go in each pen.

There are 4 pens.

Are any of your sheep missing?

Working with sheep can be hard work, but it can be fun, too! You have to like to count a lot!

Hundred Chart

1	2	3	4	5	6	7	8	9	10
11	12	13	14	15	16	17	18	19	20
21	22	23	24	25	26	27	28	29	30
31	32	33	34	35	36	37	38	39	40
41	42	43	44	45	46	47	48	49	50
51	52	53	54	55	56	57	58	59	60
61	62	63	64	65	66	67	68	69	70
71	72	73	74	75	76	77	78	79	80
81	82	83	84	85	86	87	88	89	90
91	92	93	94	95	96	97	98	99	100

What Comes Next?

Make your own hundred chart to help you count. Use different colors to show skip counting patterns. Show patterns for skip counting

- by 2.
- by 5.
- by 10.
- by 25.
- by 50.

You can count anything you see!

Now, look around you. Count something you see.

Then, look outside. Count something you see.

There is always something to count!

Glossary

count: to name numbers in order.

equal groups: groups that have the same amount.

estimate: to choose a number close to an exact amount.

greater than: more than. 4 is greater than 3.

group: like things or amounts put together, such as groups of 5.

hundred chart: a chart that shows numbers in rows of 10. The first row starts at 1. The last row ends with 100.

less than: fewer than. 5 is less than 9.

pattern: a group of things that repeats over and over. This is a letter pattern: aabbccaabbccaabbcc.

skip count: to count forward or backward by a number greater than 1. For example, you get these numbers when you skip count by 5: 5, 10, 15, 20, 25.

tally chart: a chart for showing data. For each item you count, you make one tally mark in the chart.

Further Reading

FICTION
Russell the Sheep, by Rob Scotton, HarperCollins, 2011
Sheep in a Jeep, by Nancy E. Shaw, Sandpiper, 2006
Where Is the Green Sheep?, by Mem Fox, Harcourt Children's Books, 2004
NONFICTION
Counting at Home, by Rebecca Rissman, Heinemann-Raintree, 2012
Over in the Meadow, by John Langstaff, Harcourt Brace, 1985

Additional Notes

The page references below provide answers to questions asked throughout the book. Questions whose answers will vary are not addressed.

Page 4: There are 10 sheep in the row.

Page 6: Idea 1: The next number is 6.

Page 7: Idea 3: The next number is 12. Children can skip count by 5, 10, 25, and 50.

Page 9: It is possible to make two groups of 4 and four groups of 2.

Page 10: There are 6 eggs in the carton. Children may skip count by 2 or 3.

Page 11: There are 30 eggs in all. Children may also skip count by 2, 3, 6, and 10.

Page 12: Counting by 5 is faster than counting by 1.

Page 15: 10, 20, 30, 40, 50, 60, 70, 80, 90, 100 = 100 pounds of wool in all. Caption question: Help children understand that sheep get haircuts in the spring because the weather is warm again.

Page 16: Caption question: Children may offer any number of ways of counting the sheep, including counting by one, skip counting, and keeping tallies.

Page 17: No sheep are missing. There are 50 + 50 sheep, or 100 sheep in all.

Page 18: No sheep are missing. A hundred chart makes it easy to skip count accurately. $25 + 25 + 25 + 25 = 100$.

Page 20: $25 + 25 + 25 + 25 = 100$; No sheep are missing.

Index

Content Consultant

David T. Hughes

David is an experienced mathematics teacher, writer, presenter, and adviser. He serves as a consultant for the Partnership for Assessment of Readiness for College and Careers. David has also worked as the Senior Program Coordinator for the Charles A. Dana Center at The University of Texas at Austin and was an editor and contributor for the *Mathematics Standards in the Classroom* series.

24